Roland Hindmarsh

orphan

OKELLO OCULI

orphan

modern african **LIBRARY**

East African Publishing House
Uniafric House, Koinange Street
P.O. Box 30571, Nairobi, Kenya

First published in 1968

Printed in letterpress by afropress ltd.
P.O. Box 30502, Saldanha Lane
Nairobi, Kenya

CONTENTS

for

PAN KABOHA

FLORA BIRIGENDA

JOHN TWINOMUCUNGUZI

and my sister ALIEK ATIANG

who deserve a place in the sun

I wish to thank PAN KABOHA

GEOFFREY NYONZIMA

CRISTEN TIMOTHY

FRANCIS ABURA KENE and

MALIAM APICA OTEMA

for their most inspiring friendship,

encouragement and help

PROLOGUE

*You are going to watch a village opera performed.
You will see each character walking
along a path. All paths crisscross at a
junction. An orphan boy is seated
crosslegged at the junction, writing
pictures of animals in the sand. He is
pensive. Today the people who talk in
these pages all pass through this junction.
Each of them notices the orphan boy. In
the village the problem of unnoticing is
still minimal. Each person performs a
drama for the orphan boy, and all of
them with the orphan boy perform for
you and me.*

*I offer no apologies for the many hills and valleys
and swamps you traverse. Villagers talk
a lot. In any case it is all part of the same
landscape covered all around under the
same skies of Isolation. Just remember
not to fall prey to the general epidemic,
that pull of the self greater far in force
than gravity.*

*Many of the symbols and figures used will be
strange to some readers. My excuse is
that these images are of a people with
human brains. Besides there is something
to be said for committing a crime that
Shakespeare too committed. These
symbols are essential for giving the poem
its setting.*

*To those that may feel that the decorum of poetry
has been infringed in parts of this poem,
I can only say I would feel guilty if I
backed away from a natural force that
is part of the essence of the outpouring
of the African mind.*

Illustrated by E. Christensson

okello the orphan

The woman whose breasts I sucked
Is gone to the worms!

Before we talked she went with the milk,
Cushion soothe fill of soft bellies,
Balm of unspoken yearn in screaming lips.
Born to earliness's helplessness
I found they had taken her woman to the soils.
I am only her absent existence,
Memory's lubricant
Weighted under loneliness's gall pool,
And soaked in the dew of tongues free now
In her goneness,
Only uncertain in dreams
And in debts still in the nursing of forgetful minds.
The woman whose tender care,

11

Like the termites that come when the hens
Have wiped their beaks for the day,
I missed,
Left me to the whims of kites's appetites
While she eloped with the Wild Cat.
Deaf to my screams of goodbye unintended,
She left me to the cuddle of loneliness.

When her sinews twanged and her
Trunk revulsed
And she defied the shame of dung forgotten out
In her sweat bath
Under insults of terrored midnight nerves
And clang yells of tingling metals
To pull her out of Labour's depths
And scream me into existence;
When bloody woman of my birth
Fought on the edge of Life's escarpment
To beat the challenge of her womanhood,
I thought I was important to her,
I thought she would never depart
Before we talked.
And before she saw my first teeth
Shyly bulge my slimy smooth gum !

When time-tried hands quivered under
The smoked glow in the hut of birth,
Village darkness watching on,
And the chatter of women in joy
And competition to leave the footprints
Of husbands on this thorny Path
In my name;

12

And the old man
Peered through his worried wrinkles,
Time's stamp on his face once smooth
When he first arrived at the clan,
Seat of worried shepherd,
And whispered yet another time:

> "He is one of us — from the Ancestors —
> The Ancestors have come to us again —
> Call him Okello — he told the twins
> To come and allow his turn too —
> Okello, we offer you these hands
> When we are still around — come —
> Okello, suck your mother — grow up to bury us !"

I hoped
My blood red clan blood,
My ears not of the dog cleansing children's
Fouls for mothers,
My spine not the grass behind the hut:
No public utility for all types !

When the goats bleated and sneezed
And hooves rumbled in the kraal
As I fell out,
I thought I had a place on the Path,
Another complementary in the juggling towards
The bewitching flames in the west,
Lures as the *Ngunydeng* wild cat's anus to hens in search,
Persuasive of purpose in the stubborn silence
Beyond the darkness after the flames have folded the trap.

I thought my mother would show me to the Path
And shake off the first dews

And pull off the thorns fond of my delicate
Uncertain feet,
But she left me to stumble on stubble
And scream tears dry off my eyes
Along the Path, alone !
Away with the Wild Cat
She left my screams to frighten nibbling
Rats under bushes
And cork ears of grazing cows,
Cows mixing waves of appetite and jolts.
The woman of my birth left
To find out the secret behind the west
Jostled away from the echoes of the questions
In my screams;
Away from the questions deep beneath the embracing
Stars in my virgin eyes
She hurried to the crowd, hurried like termites
Lured to fires invading the grip of peaceful darkness;
Fires leading to the solidarity in the collective
Deaths in the cooking pot of trappers,
And into the depth of the emptiness beyond the glow
From between the cooking stones,
And the blank behind false currency notes.
In between the walls of unheeding,
And generations of gullibility,
She rushed to the false hopes of romance with
The Wild Cat in the western glow.
Unheeding the secret in the talk
Of the drums,
Tickler of breasts,
And the message in the chat of fermenting
Beer in midnight rumination,
Of the honey throbbing in young men's thighs

And trickling in silent protests of unfulfilment
In exhausted veins of the elders;
She uprooted the *Okono* plants of her woman
From the old homestead.
Only to find the new home in ashes
And built of deaf walls of darkness.

She was only my mother by reference,
Leaving me a reference
To face alone
The darkness hidden below the glare of
The mid-day sunshine;
To grimace and coil in cold pain
Under the pools of shadows of foul breaths
Of brats;
Gasping questions about Ancestors, and
Clan elders's welcomes, and mothers,
In between my sobs!

grandmother of okello's father's clan

You see — your mother was married —
The cows came from this house —
Your father was poor
And so we said these cows — why don't
You find a girl!
And he found your mother — that woman!
And I remember my bull —
And my daughter a good girl and they had
Married her well — those people married!
And your mother, I told your people — that
Child is good, you drive the cows.
She came,
But before she could stay
The child of the bride price of my womb,
Mirror of my proof,

17

Was eloped away by the earth.
I sang my goodbyes unsaid in the moment
Of her sleep and dawn of stench
Perfume of my galled heart.
I sang to the sleep in the village,
To the music of the rains and the hum of
The grasses along the path to the well
But the urine in my bladder still ached
For release and I knew even
Starvation in the stomach of a baby
Never recovers spilled milk from the
Throats of the compound soil.
She passed here with the haste of love
From young lusts at wooing,
Real in the reality of unreality
And lasting in unlastingness.
But she left you,
To speak for her and plead with
The cows in your uncles' kraal to suckle their
Calves and release the milk in their udders.
You will mend the crack in the walls
And quieten the protest in my wrinkled flaps,
And I can sleep again.
You are of us, my intestines, my husband!

okello's mother's uncle

You see — your mother — my sister —
She built this house. With the cows for
Her woman she married this woman.
This house and this woman are yours.
Of all my sisters that girl
Always sent me away song-boasting
The bull of our clan and the
Fertility of my mother to the village.
I scorned the skies and challenged the
Dumb soil on the path to outshout the
Beer in my stomach. But I soon learnt of the
Bee sting in honey-heavy honey comb!
My sister had no fire between her buttocks
When she had food in her house.
Her hands were bitter

And woke the spirits dormant in your spine
With the bite of the beer of her hands.

My sister lived in the belch off many stomachs
Her smile killed thirst in throats
And crackled smoked knees defying their
Last resolution to let the rope
Go over the line to Death's victory tug.
But who has found the secret of
Trapping satisfaction in the stomach
And making the wet raw log
Win the floating duel against the dry log?
The pests leave behind
The cows with the dry udders in the kraal
And the rains listen to the cauldron mumbles
And growls in the wizard's hut, and laugh
At the thirsty whispers from the roots of
Crops. And famine does not save seeds for sowing
Or face the chill of morning dews.
But when the marriage is over and the feasters
Have gone,
The empty silence in the home
And the dead bones' stories
And the yawn in the granaries
Silence the rumble beat of the drums
And the chatter voices only in *your* ears!
And you are here now my nephew.
My sister's child
My sister's blood,
You have come to us from your people
To look at us.
When you are still rubbish like this
Who swallows saliva on you!

The insides of a cow in its dung coating
Tickle and dilate no nose!
Stay here with these little fellow animals
In the homestead,
These fellows with running noses and swollen
Bellies.
Weaning men out of little devils shrivels
The old men's buttocks
But water has no teeth,
No axe to scrape the hard rocks as it sings
And laps on its ways;
And the soft sole of a foot soon carves a path
To the well.
Your stomach cannot level the ridges in these
Hands and break the backs of the bullocks
In the shed.

village gossip

That woman looks like a stump;
She eats as if her teeth are in her stomach,
As if she is throwing the food past her head,
She closes her anus with her heels
At a beer party in other's homes
But has *Ocecu* bird's eyes
And steams from between her backside
When she has food in her house;
That woman whose womb was made slippery
By people's sons in youth
And now loathes other women's children
In her barrenness;
That woman who sees all moons
And has the bark of dogs and the bleat of
Goats and the dance songs of fires
In full glow for company

And dreams the hoots of owls and the yell
Of jackals for the scream of babies
Twisting in sleep;
That woman who hides the faeces of others'
Children among her vegetables
And has trapped the fertility of many women
In her dark charcoal eyes,
And tied up the power of the spear of many
Young men with herbs from her wizard mother;
That woman who thinks she will
Never laugh the whiteness of her
Teeth to the worms in the soil,
Killed your mother!
She broke medicine in her feet
Because your mother did not puff up in bed
And salt her food
With soils from graves; because your mother
Stank of the vomit of children
And did not sleep from lighting fires amid
The midnight screams and sighs
Of little bodies scared of the
Sinister welcome smile of Death!
She helped your mother out of the
Troubled looks in children's eyes
And the sting of little nails
With unintended pain from careless scratch holds;
From milky smiles oozing off smooth plains
And muddy small feet assumingly imposed
On mothers,
She wanted to save her!
From the ridicule of the struggle with Death

To bear destined travellers to compound Death's mirage dance
In the sunset glow,
Out of the tangle of seed the mother and
Child of plant, and plant-child and mother
Of seed: dying of birth in mutual
Toil to postpone the day of total disintegration
She chose to save her!
That woman with a dark heart exiled
The woman who bore you, from the village.

village elder

Are you around?
Stopping to wonder takes a strain
And the stop is a surprise.
I do not hear your wails;
The sap flow in the tree trunk
Bypasses the withering branch,
And the flamboyant bloom in the flowers
Unnotices the thirst to death
Of a leaf.
I see you quiver from the roots of your body;
Your eyes well out waters
But I don't hear your sobs. The tethered goat's
Appeal for release from the chill
Of rain-drench is faster to my ears,
And I puzzle why it puzzles you.
Your hand wanders past the meal calabash,

You walk past the hut door;
When other children dance to the warm
Satisfaction in their stomachs after a meal,
You drowse in placid dream
And the long stare in your eyes is loose,
Engulfing all in unnoticing.
You are not here.
Your taproot is cut in the soil
In a terrifying betrayal
And a final condemnation of your fibrous roots
To shallow-lain juices.
Those awakening to the fragility
Of life and the eagerness of the pangs
Below the surface,
Groan on Death's calculated scratches
While lovers sigh
Knees rubbing
Cheeks melting and cooling
In the sag and thrust of billowing,
Loving and searching
In the woods of copulation;
And the *Awele* bird koos through
The poignant silence and brood of leaves
At mid-day tropical siesta;
And a hen dusts its feathers in acted dissociation
From under submission to a cock's climb.
The courting grasshopper chirps in a sun bath
Oblivious to the pangs in the body
Of a vagabond dog dragging along
Against the weight of creeping rot in a limb.
Trapped within the walls of localised awareness,

Nature's imposition to justify her
Indifference to individual pains
And denial of special treatment to each
Caught alone within isolation's sound proof walls
All move within unbridged selves
And the ethic of indifference accepted in
Resigned imitation.

The message in the yell of the goat
Frightened of the vision behind the slaughter,
The glassy light in its eyes — unfinished
Beams left bouncing off the rude opacity
Of the sudden wall of void eternity;
The melancholy chat of flesh in the cooking pot:
Only arouse all appetites for heed.
The disposed-of bones in the homestead,
Scattered in a jumble, question the fate of
The flesh that once walled their unity
And sing the credo of the final isolation...

Orphan boy, you must learn to expect little
From the generosity of the world,
To grapple alone with the top of the earth,
As the baby must will to walk
And teach its wobbly feet the harsh
Truth of hunters,
And of young courters and men
Whose wives other men do not
Knock on the grass
To pay the food the women have begged;
That the world laughs
At idle wishers that dread pain
To earn a desired good.

The man who wants his manhood back
To sleep from the stings
Of women's scorpion tongues
Always calling him "woman, woman",
Bears the shame of the return
To a baby in the hut,
To sit naked on his mother's forest
And cleanse off the shyness
That catches his man
When a woman opens her thighs
To provoke the spirits of his fathers
In him
With that food of foods
That needs no cooking.

My child, listen!
The toils of this earth
Have no owner.
The fat as pregnant hippos,
The short as a leper's toes,
The tall as the *abir* sorghum
And the thin as the mosquito thigh
That are the source of village mourners
When dysentery visits us;
Those that boast of wealth
And beauty they never won
Nor gave themselves in wombs
And those that suffer from ugly looks.
All know
Happiness is no kinsman
No twin brother to share a termite's head with.

They know suffering is life's
Smile in the dark,

Fought with the omen of struggle
From the blood omen.
And when this world's ills come
To the bitter bodied,
They multiply like an *Oro* bush fire
Or April grasshoppers in the millet garden;
But only the *Apele* man
Whose muscles only flex
To carry the kill of other men home,
And the woman who brews her husband
Dung for beer and roasts him
Jiggers for simsim, crumble and die on self pity
When the things of this earth
Serve us tendons for meal
And blunt the blade of the digging hoe!

Poverty of the man without cows for a wife,
The man with no sisters
With udders and breasts for horns,
The man whose mother's womb
Smelt not of the odour of a kraal
Bears the stench of many salivas
In search of cows and the pillar of a hut.
Women whose compounds are blessed
With a kraal
Say his walk is clumsy
Like the snake in the newly
Ploughed field,
His teeth project out of his
Mouth like a warthog's
And he crawls in walking as
If yaws fill between his buttocks.
They insult him that his

Wake up, orphan!
Wake from the null of the cold pain
In your mutilated taproot;
Wake, and wade through the mist
Over your eyes. Be a man.
Walk to a spear
And learn the message of facing, alone,
The twang of its stem and the silent
*   power*
In its blade;
Rise to face isolation's challenge
In the dance arena
At the teasing charge of a girl's
*   beckoning*
Breasts, swinging in the "get fixed"
*   dance*
In moonlight

Body is cold with the shadow
Spirits of dead wizards who were
His uncles,
And that his skin is taut and dry
As if the back side of a penis bore him!
Children who travel to the ginnery
In lorries taking cotton
Compare his base
To those of the Indian merchants
And say his millet meal pieces
Behind him are dry as the cassava
Slices left in the heat of the December sun!

The poor boy with no cows
Hears but does not listen
And wipes each and all to the back of his head.
He curbs his tail like the hungry
Dog to a master.

Though his tongue be full of
The venom of the *Kalalang* ant, or
Sharp as the penis of the *Obia* grass
And ready with foul words
As fat people with broken wind;
A poor boy in begging
Cowers like a castrated bull
And tightens his ribs to weather
The stench of the price of borrowed
Marriage!
He weeps his soul on the shrine
Of sweat and muscle
As the hyena reaps from the field
Of shamelessness!

34

And hoards in the granary of patient silence
And time.
My son, the sun is not
Always dead at midnight
And fire does not always beget ash!

Wake up, orphan!
Wake from the null of the cold pain
In your mutilated taproot;
Wake, and wade through the mist
Over your eyes. Be a man.
Walk to a spear
And learn the message of facing, alone,
The twang of its stem and the silent power
In its blade;
Rise to face isolation's challenge
In the dance arena
At the teasing charge of a girl's beckoning
Breasts, swinging in the "get fixed" dance
In moonlight;
Ripe breasts of youth
Daring you to her loving body
Boiling and steaming opiums of passion
From rhythmic tremors,
Melting and rippling perfumed motions
With and towards the depth
Of the heave and talk of drums in melodious
Self rendering;
Drums yearning to pour out all
In a final act of self-fulfilment.

Dancing to dissolve herself
In the honey of rhythmic intoxication,

Vibrating, on and on, to annihilate her
Being in the ether of the orgasm at
The fusion ground of melody and the spirit
In her yearning for the depths of realisation.
Challenging all being around her
With her fire,
Knowing even the heavens will not exhaust
Her power;
Calling on the skies and the bowels of the
Forests
To behold the ripples of the waves
In her liquid buttocks, melting
With the advancing provocation of drum waves
Bashing the shores of her body in moonlight
Dance.
Wake, to stand the echo
And cold vibrations in your bowels
When the roar of the wounded lion thunders
And quakes all around;
Face the dark eyes of ultimate loneliness
At the surge of a lion's angry mass
In the *Arum* hunt wilderness:
Ridiculing, dissolving man's being
Under the advancing darkness of its upright
Charge behind its aimed paw
And challenged mountain rage.
Orphan boy, wake and face life's
Twisted humour!

Wake out of the soothe of tranquillisers,
Sympathy, love,
Thin delicate threads for bridges across
The chasms and walls of silence

Between letters in an alphabet,
Between bricks in a wall claiming unity
In sharing layers of cement and asserted
Brickness fragmented to satisfy identity,
Deriving a unity in the distributed presence
In the wall's expanse;
A fragile unity that crumbles in violent
Confusion and panic at the tease of an
Earthquake's casual belch,
And falling back to calls of sympathy
And the oneness in walls.
But,
Who can feel the pains of the woman who
Has no children, who refuses to bear?
And the father who follows the slayers
Of his son, a following,
Knowing the death of a son, like the rain
Spear,
Will never be ransomed!
Who can see the pangs of the girl
Whose guardian spirit left
The gods to spit their oil of wrath, leprosy,
On her young body?
Or see the intensity of the bitings
Of the disease that makes a child
Cry incessantly in the middle of the sun!
What doors can sympathy and love open?
My son, tragedy is not a marriage feast
To which people flock in broad daylight;
Come with broad eyes
That know no shame
And ears which as for hearing insults
And grumbles accompanying pots of beer

Released to intruders to the feast,
They hear
But plug their ears
And remind the hosts, and the greedier
Guests,
That when the guinea fowls are gone back
To the bush,
The hens remain loyal,
And the sun gives each hill
Its turn of warm gayness.

Men and women brought by their stomachs
Fill the home of marriage feasting;
Relatives and those making relations
To back demands,
Intruders, some shy, some with heads
Hardened to shame;
And all the women remember whatever
The hosts borrowed once
And debts a dead relative left unpaid,
The illness their medicine cured once;
In-laws of all degrees
Cross streams, and walk paths through many
Villages
To come to drink back some of the hospitality
Taken out of them once,
And feel special,
And drink, and drink!

And in the towns where people
Come with Invitation Cards
To enter the place of drinking
Bottled beers and bitter alcohols

38

Of many kinds from foreign lands,
And all the former lovers
Of the bride
Also get Cards in the guise of
Cousins, brothers and nephews.
And they come to remember
How they initiated her
And broke the cover of her youth
And swam in the ooze of her inner life
Before she learnt to conceal the fatigue in her deflated body
With hollow sighs and false cheers
And keep remembering to call out
The right name in the cheers!
And the naughty among them
Want a last wink, becoming bolder
With more alcohol
And smiling easily with the glee of
A second-hand car dealer
Mocking the excitement of a customer
Inheriting other's stale rejects.
And those disillusioned with
Their own marriages,
Say how happy they are
To be invited to such an expensive
Wedding, drinking hurriedly,
And drunk women
Urinate freely from between expensive
Dresses,
And throw sex recklessly at young men
In defiance of husbands,
And compare details of wedding shows
Forever,
Recalling their own false excitement once.

And everybody remembers
To register congratulations, unmeant;
And to comment favourable things
On the looks and dress of the bride
And check on the quantity of alcohol.
The VIPs, or Very Impotent Persons
Who drive big cars and big stomachs,
Know they are wanted as part of the
Decorations; decorations bought bitterly
By couples of low standing.
They bring wives who talk loudly
Shouting to shout their desire to be
Noticed and known as the women who
Sleep with the important men,
And to argue the acceptance of their looks
With the price of their dresses, wigs, ornaments,
And the intensity of the erosion
On their faces, and of the shrieks they
Scratch from floors with High Heels.
And the man of medicine concludes:

Young man, you have brought new
Nerves to be hit, tossed, tested,
Taught and surprised to a deadening;
To drain out its passions
Till even generating sympathy is a problem
And nothing is tragic any more.

Come to discover we are all impotent
Mourners on a bed-side,
Aware of the futility of understanding
The pains in the patient each of us is;
Incapable communicants always falling
Inwards to ourselves

Like the widow worried about suitors'
Tastes, on her husband's deathbed;
Afraid of the real face of the flash
Of pangs in our spirits at the sight of
Suffering,
Like lovers afraid of the hypocrisy
Of passing eroticism for love of the
Sex catalyst.

Learn the alphabet of life,
That we are born with the indelible
Sin of Isolated Selves,
To remain perpetual tourists
To each other
Along life's pathways!

Always remember the ritual song
Of our wise men of medicine
When washing off the ill omen
Of the ghosts of disgruntled elders
Off the birth luck of young women.
The song old women,
Young girls,
Husbands,
Chant in melancholy arrogance
Under the *Abila* shrine to the dead,
Goes like this:

> *I have a right to be*
> *I esteem myself highly*
> *I came from the womb of a woman*
> *Before the false morning glows*
> *Before the reddening of the horizon*

Not from a cursed marriage because
My mother did not elope
I must have come for a purpose, not
Of your making
I must have come for a reason higher
Than your usage, for you did not design
My coming and the world
It is no prerogative of yours
To reject or
Accept me
Leave me alone to live my turn.
For you
I exist.

woman whose husband is of okello's clan

Today Okello! Tomorrow **Okello!**
Every day *'Otwaca'* wants food,
Scrape the bottom of the pot
Woman of the house!
And I trouble these bones till
I am fat as a squashed frog dry on a road.
Where does the food go, you my people!
Should I cook these withered hands
For Okello's stomach's hunger!
My man where is the food?
You talk like a visitor,
Like one ignorant of the emptiness
In the granaries
And of the famine in this home.
You talk as if you do not hear the

43

Feast dance of the rats in the
Millet granary
And do not see the bite of hunger
In the flat eyes of the children.
Feeding my own will kill me.
Where shall I find the body
For feeding other people's children?
The four ears of millet now left
I shall keep for seed.
Last season anybody's daughter spat
On my face as I begged for seed
And I was scum and talk of the village!
Hunger and bitterness of heart
Are no monopoly of Okello.
Who has not seen toil and been the child of
Poverty?
Who has not used her nails to scratch
Hard at the earth!
I weep here night long from my back
While he sleeps soundly,
And the back aches, people,
As if it would come off my body next day!
At least people care for Okello.
But who cares for my type?
Even if they see disease drying
You dry and the sinews of your neck,
Once soft and swaying always,
Who cuts sleep on you ?
Suffering is for us all,
Do not bother my sick ears with another's
Burdens.
I was born of other people's blood,
Okello has his people;

I did not kill his mother
And no spirits of the dead will haunt me!

His mother ran away to leave the burden
To whom?
Not me. I refuse. Whose body is bitter?

When Okello joins the clan
Of "yes, no" people he will
Say he is going to the Office
On my funeral day.
Where will he find the hands to carry
My dirty wrinkled village body
To the grave?
Where would be the soap, the dettol
To wash off my smell from his suit,
And the polish to cleanse off the
Grave soil from his "Made
In Italy" shoes?
If he came to my funeral
Where would the village people
Find chai and coffee
And cook Lunch, and Dinner and Breakhunger
For his prostitute Secretary,
Giggling drainer of salaries before wives
See anything brought home?

Where will the girl of the big men
Sleep? The girl who wives equals
Of her father and grandfather
To sleep on a soft bed and cook
With elec-fire and see T.V.
Bought by big men using her on hire

And complaining to wives daily
Of the high increase of taxes!
Where will she find the ears
For addresses that don't "Miss" her
Father's name, baptising her with
Education's civilising waters?
A man's name stuck on her
Because sweet native names are primitive,
Meaning laden names like:

> *Song of the rain*
> *God's sweet one*
> *Our God is alive*
> *Tingling honey*
> *Laughing clouds*
> *Food of my soul*

Names that are the record of the pulse
Of our hearts at the shrine of birth
When the navel is cut and the nipple's
Yearn for sucking is answered!
The girl wooed with big money
And big things,
Has fragile life and will be
Poisoned by food from roughened hands
Taken for dirt
And calabashes condemned to automatic
Filth for not coming from factories.
The food that nourished the man
Whose car she now moons in, would
Kill her,
And she would not return to the town
Where big men of Office trample on

Daring young men who touch the cow
Of the big bull,
And cut each other's throats in
Jobs and politics for her body!

Okello will come to speak English
On us,
And bring tourists to take notes at
My funeral, and capture our shadows
In machines for money.
We shall all become things back here,
Easy treasures for politicians to
Use as they choose
And lead to the slaughter house
For ransom in their quarrels.
Okello's car-clan will come to
Wrestle on our backs and construct
Swimming pools to fill with the blood
Of the "great unwashed" and of heathens
From "Education" and "Massitics".
We shall be Gentiles of their
Religion of the Looting of the Blacks,
By the Black Bastards, for Becoming
Black-Purples!
Leave me alone to observe the last of
The world left for me.
Have I not been cheated enough
To deserve a pity?
Have not men of sacrifice
And the Other World, proclaimed, and sang,
Grown pot-bellied while I watched
Eggs and foods leave our homes for missions?
Have I not watched men and hooded women

Have I been deaf to the giggles,
And long whispers in the ritual of
"Self Shaming" when girls and young
*   wives*
Say their sins while the man in the
*   cassock*
Counts the beads on her waist and
Fingers the tips of her nipples,
His eyes reddening?

Of Love of the white Big
Man with a beard, in the Clouds,
Beat the barrenness in their wombs
And their holy testicles out of other
People's children?

Have I been deaf to the giggles,
And long whispers in the ritual of
"Self Shaming" when girls and young wives
Say their sins while the man in the cassock
Counts the beads on her waist and
Fingers the tips of her nipples,
His eyes reddening?

When a young girl leaves
Singing love songs
On the grinding stone
To sing grave songs of strange
People of strange tongues,
And takes her breasts to ripen in
The catechism chorus rituals,
And reports of the scratch of rough beards
Of sacrifice on her *shea*-butter smooth
Cheeks,
Am I blind to the wizardry of the crucified
Witch doctor?
Have I not seen our medicine men
Called witches all,
Called black agents to blackness,
Because they did not write papers
And call themselves "civilised",
And their cures "miracles",
And did not go out of their lands

50

To insult other people's Witch Doctors?
I have been fooled long enough.
Let me rest now!

Let me not remember
The spirit of my sister
That wanders in shame without a shrine
In her memory because hooded women from within
Virginity Walls,
Women that feared the wrath of husbands,
Tied rosaries around our necks!

Let me forget those tears
That dried off my eyes,
Tears for my dead father,
Killed by desecrators of the shrines to our
Ancestors,
Sorrow tears I denied his spirit high in the
Winds,
Because we turned to squeeze out sorrows
To a chalk figure on a Cross,
Tried to act out sorrows and self desecrations
Told in oracles heard
In far away lands!

Travelling agents of other people's witch
Doctors have bedevilled me long enough,
Made us all sleepers in tricksters' lands
And led us to plains of confusion,

Without trails to the past
And shelter in the chilly present.
Ashamed of our real selves in past thoughts,

Uneasy in stale presents,
Awkward like out-of-water is for fish,
Yet trapped in the hollow selves of sour-sweet
Present;
Present of racing to catch our inner selves
Unlooking at the patchwork of modernity
We frenzy to erect on the outside
To silence the nagging shame and protesting
Void below the surface;
Eating and eating our insides out,
Insides revulsing under the patchwork of
Fur-coats and Limousines and dejuiced accents;
Corroding our insides,
Sapping our spines,
To race further and further into the desert
Of Isolation
And receive the baptism of class clans.
People! I have seen enough of the
Mass mutilation of my people
By the men of the Chalk Figure on a Cross,
Enough of the betrayal of erected illusions.
Let me not chase more mirages
Through Okello's future!

The labour of my ribs
And of my freckled hands, were robbed
By brothers of the Preachers
Of the "Saviour", come to us
With messages we were to see, slowly.
The thorns on the head of the Chalk Figure
Had come to prick and prod
Our men: in prisons, and the mines and
Farms of the Preachers' kinsmen.

52

The magicians' candles burned;
Black and red robes paraded on altars,
Platforms of omens;
In the Shrines made of bricks, Churches,
Big ornamented shrines,
They uttered enchantments, and we sang with
Them,
Unknowing they chanted to their Witch Doctor
To ward off the anger of our Ancestors
That mourned and seared to revenge
For themselves and us!

Men and boys
Taken away from our homes,
Came home husks of humanity.
They returned "Bloody fuckined",
"Demeted", "Tanboyed" and
"Bladifooled";
Raped of the power of their muscles
In the name of "taxes", that is,
Returns for the altruism of our civilisers,
Or, bluntly,
Maintainance fees for the soldiers and
Workers of the Termite Queens
Palaced across seas.

And the cassocked and collared magicians
Drank wine on their shrine pedestal
Amid candle fire,
Uttering more sayings, sometimes with belches,
And pronounced oracles from dead men's
Land, far away behind the clouds,
Promising rewards for bearing the raking

Of our people's bodies
And the rotting and floggings in the prisons
And tunnels of mines.
Powders and herbs were burnt to the spirits
Of the dead clansmen and women
Of the magicians, whose names they gave us,
And prayed, and told us to pray,
To their ghosts to sweeten our wretched fates.

Our men came home shoulder stooped
And talked fast
To hide the insults eating the depths
Of their spirits
And the haunt of the undared out compulsions
To kill and hit out,
Burning urges that filled their souls.
And when they died on return, when they could,
We bought the enchantments of the cassocked
Magicians
To appease their spirits gone with protests!
I have seen things, people!
Be content to let me observe things
In my aloneness!

Leave me alone.
The Constitution says I should be left alone
Because I am ignorant, diseased and poor
And other people must think for me.
It says I cannot see,
That I am blind and cannot notice the growth
Of buttocks and bellies of those
Who think for me and my lot.
That I am deaf and cannot hear the growl

Of the big dogs over the spoils
And the kill.
It is said I did not run in chase when the
The beast was speared,
And that after all my plots were not
Ravaged by the beast they speared and killed.

Their catechism of rule says
That I did not speak English to the beast
But only chanted and danced at rallies,
When the campaign and the hunt cry to the
Kill still included my lot
And we too were still counted with
The victims of exploitation:
When we still needed to be liberated.
It says I did not issue statements to
Cry against the scratches of the beast;
That now that the animal had fallen
I have no qualifications,
No qualified knives for skinning
And no cocktail robes for collecting the streaming blood!

All of them in the Exclusive Club
Are allergic to my village simplicity,
To my crude pride in myself and my nativity,
Because they are all anxious to tell, to
Shout out to their former despisers
Who *gave* them verbal pride
Called Independence,
That they are not primitive,
And do not sleep in huts or on trees,
And do not eat with their fingers
But with iron and metal things,

55

Each one eating from a separate plate
For fear of other's greed and appetite;
That their skins do not smell of
Animal hides and of fresh leaves but
Of Paris or London fabrics bought
From foreign merchants:
"Vat you vant Sir — vich thing — this one —
No! — take this — very good quality —
Not from India — made in England, Sir —
I sell it you very cheap as
A friend — vat your last prize — this only
One left in my stock — new fashion just
Arrived — vant it? — And vat else Sir? —
I bring only good quality for your type! —
See this — very good for you — try it and see."

Foreign merchants who loot in glee
And always are first on Donation lists
And compete in sending presents to the big
Bulls.

The big bulls and their henchmen say
I am ignorant and cannot see that it is
Hell to be at the top.
But I know it to be so now because I see
They now have a life to fear for
And a new cowardice has struck them,
The cowardice that makes a thief's eye loose,
That bottom coldness
That makes impotent husbands tremble all over
At a wife's frank touch of the boil
In a quarrel,
And release a violence on to her,

A cruelty of a mad dog in ecstatic therapy,
A viciousness and angry sweat
That yells out but cannot
Heal the wound inflicted deep on
His manhood!
Cruelty opened out in the blackout
Of the oblivion and drunken forgetfulness
Of a suicide case
Struggling against the increasing choke
Of drowning!

I see it all!
But they do not see that I see.
They do not want to see that I see them
And I see through them
And through their lies and propaganda.
The impotent man does not want to see
That others do not believe
His stories of felling many women;
The ugly girl refuses to accept
The cold story of mirrors,
And a poor teacher shouts and terrorises
Against the cold silent despise in the
Eyes of pupils, refusing to hear
The message in the whispers and
Sobs of his victims.

A Faller-into-Privileged Looting
Refuses to see the sneer
And the accusations
In acted submissions of Office Boys,
"Boys" condemned to their "For-Spitting-On"
Clan,

By the tattoo marks of no-qualifications
And "Who knows your father?"
Written on the walls of their foreheads!

Do as the oracle of the Constitution says:
Let sleeping natives lie,
Alone with their poverty, disease and ignorance!
Husband!
Give me a place in the sun, to breathe!
Let your orphan nephew ponder the saying:
"God helps those who help themselves".

okello's age-mate

Okello, my age mate,
I saw the fire in Atim's eyes
And the looseness and limp flexibility
In her neck;
I watched the awkward rumble of adolescent
Femininity burst out of her body
In uncoordinated excitements,
Dissolving her into a shy chance beauty,
Innocent flames in her body
Reaching out tongues
In strange jerks of eagerness;
Dancing out clutches and drives toward
Felt out firewood on you
For an embrace to a consumption
And total fusion in a synthesis unto ashes
In an all-out plunge to cross frontiers.
Your sap, now felt in her veins,

Sing out of her lonesome neck, poised neck
Balancing a water pot with a sophistication,
Intensely sublime,
Out of the pure rawness in her virgin body;
Jutting her neck decidedly above
And oblivious to the tease hiss of grasses
Along the well path;
Neck in abandon,
Arguing her feminine vulnerability,
And the helplessness to a pluck
Of a beautiful flower in bloom!
But I see the sulk in your face
And awkward shyness heating pimples
On your face.
I know the mushrooms are still coy below
The soils,
Slowly nudging the arrogant refusal of the
Soils,
Writing the liberation songs
And chanting the Harambee melody to a chorus
Provoking germs of strength in collective
Madness,
Before the final explosion out of
The suppression and suffocation under the
Malicious glee of soil strata.
But I know,
The date of outburst and assertion will come.

Let us go and dare the bush ghosts
With our youth,
And tease the guardian shadows of bird with
Traps;

ithful for the husband's
...ing votes;
...pound their wives' chests
...ed all the tears and saliva
to see the shoes, and ties a...   ake
...politics
...vist their necks   out
...ists willing to the itchy
...f the men of politics
...f taking them to the big meeting
...y bulls at the meeting
...e the big men of the party
...n far away and going by lorry
...rful dresses given by the big
...men before whom you swing and
...and flap your breasts and break
...ng home to be yours,
...n must stand up for their rights!
...en must be emancipated, our women
...ated from the morality of e village
...n resisting the lust of the men
...e big men,
...se grey beards and stale liquids
...e guns of the young girls and
...and hot young bodies,
...e the big old men pant like dogs
...ed! in the name of public service ...

Invade the ill omens protecting mango fruits
In ripening season.
The soles of your feet never get worn out
Their resistance and stubborn endurance
Angers bush thorns to a strange ferocity;
Thorns getting sicker and thirstier
For blood,
Unseeing the path of the pains to the base
Of victims' necks,
Unbelieving that they can ever suffer.

Let us live out ourselves
Before the sun sets again
And sleep cajoles and lulls us to the mercy
Of the witch doctors of Darkness;
To wake, having refused lures and traps
To the way of surrender into final
Disintegration and the petrifaction
Of our insides;
Having returned with new vigours and
Ammunitions for kicking out more,
Again!

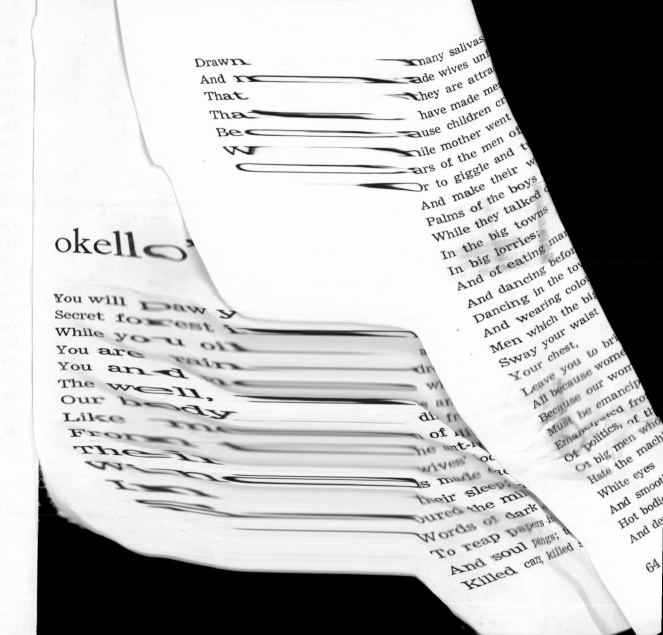

The insults, the insults and venom
From your mouth;
The rudeness in your head can make a slave
Girl miscarry;
You can make men hurt themselves in the *Arum* hunt;
The smoke from your mouth
Is the broken wind of dead wizards!
You talk bitter like the man of politics
After the papers of hatred have put him among the lions of
    government
Whose democracy leads the way for him,
Whose justice,
The justice from people's taxes,
Is bursting his navel buttons
And deflating his buttocks
And recalling his man.

Like the man of politics you carry
Bad sayings about me
At the tip of your bottom hole,
To get your wants!
Like those men of rule you will
Open your wives' thighs,
To men of what you crave.
I am sick; your father must
Find another slave girl,
My husband must find the woman
Whom the spirits of the dead love!
Men never get finished,
My girlhood can still make the throats
Of men roll saliva.
When I walk to the market
Stumps on the path feast on the

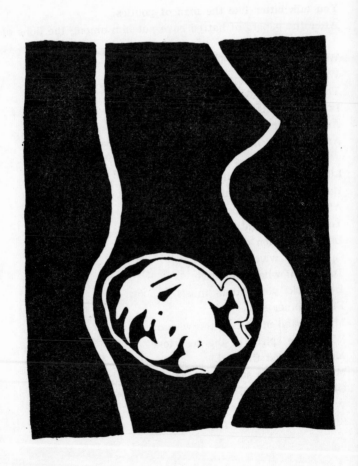

Pregnancy is not a shameful accident,
And the   flowers of my womb are not
    dead statistics,
Waking to pass water from gallons of
    alcohol
Other than waking to the cry
Of the child who has urinated in a dream!

Toes of men caught stealing looks
At my swaying waist and my
Waist markings.
When I break wind under the beer
Party the men do not spit.
My sob of cheer still draws hot streams off
Tingling spines
And my grip of womanness holds.
Men never get finished. My husband is not
The only man.
The hills of my womb have not been denuded
By the white man's pills; the medicines of
Death have not corroded my womb; my womb
Has never been a coffin, never been a
Cauldron of mutilations, never a grave for
A baby from the medicines of civilisation!
My womb is pure: I have never been a walking
Carrier of death; a giggling gas chamber of
Anybody's baby;
I have never carried folded socks
Whose milk is galled by medicines
Known from learning!
The fertility of my womb shall never
Enrich dustbins and public utilities
With abortions done for fashion;
Nor drank from men throwing money in
The place of buying drunkenness, bars,
Men in the auction for your body.

Pregnancy is not a shameful accident,
And the flowers of my womb are not dead statistics,
Waking to pass water from gallons of alchohol

Other than waking to the cry
Of the child who has urinated in a dream!

I am not like the woman of town,
The woman of emancipation,
Of the place of the devil fire of no flames,
The epileptic fire;
I am not the woman of town love
Who celebrates the latest abortion, with the
Alcohol of machines from Chemists,
On the laps of the abortion's father!
My cow hoof, my drainage trench,
My moon trail,
The passage of what I am, and
The route of my sanity,
This stamp of my womanhood is no interest-laden
Loan from the Good Spirit.
Who has ever sold a mouth to a tooth brush seller?

The instruments of holy noise in towns,
Those machines that trap singing ghosts
That they call radio, T.V.;
Those running metals of death called cars
And lorries;
The sweetness of their noise does not make
The milk in my breast bite
Like the sudden scream of the seed
Of my womb who has just hurt himself
In play.
The whispers of envy and admiration,
The talk of other women about those things,
Does not elate my body;
My body shadow does not awake, jolt

Like the body shadow of a cow in scent of danger,
And the ears of my womanhood remain cold deaf.

Kars and radiu cannot dig the grave
For one's dead body, nor
Fold and place you correctly in the grave;
Radiu cannot radiu you a grandchild
To bother your old bones
And urinate on your wrinkled body on the way to
Planting cassava in the fields beyond the grave!
The woman of town smears the furrows
Of decay;
The woman of civilisation plasters
The cracks on the wall;
She bribes the informers from
Decay, and the receding trails of youth,
With a hyena white wash called kocmatik,
And sweetened marrows of dead men,
Marrows sold in rich shops.

I do not need the white man's herbs of youth
To skin out beckoning youth in retreat.
Who can prevent the march of age!
My herb of youth is the after-noon
Sun on the gentle *yao* oil on my smooth blackness,
The gentle *yao* oil
Shining on the entrance to my thigh
Is what gets my cock to lift its head
To probe a crow from the skies
And to do the pride dance around me.

When the way to my thigh shines
My man calls me to pick a grass piece

From his eye!
When it shines from the gentle *yao* oil
When I am cooking my food
And my man says he can see his face on my thigh,
He makes us sleep without eating.

I do not need corrosive liquids,
Nor pills of defoliation,
No heart rendering complexion patches
From medicines
Of courting the impolite hands of age's decay!

My children do not eat soaked beans
Because their mother spends all in the house
To buy youth in bottles,
To enemies of the wrinkles around the eye corners,
And the approaching waves on the forehead,
And the crevasses — canals from
The stem of the nose to the swamp
Shores of the mouth,
And brisk waves in between the fingers;
Old age cracks us
Like the pot
Spoilt in the fire,
The pot of a woman of unlucky hands;
The sun will catch you with setting
Before you mend it,
And the water in that pot will never be
Used for cooking that night,
And the leaked-out water
And the Path will sooner want the pot away from you!

The disease of dogs the soldiers brought
From Ethiopia, and Burma and white
   women,
The disease they brought from the war
That eats and rots the womb
That makes men leak and rats eat the
Front of their trousers

And the day will have gone,
And the work will have been undone
And the pot will not have arrived home
And the pot will not be
To plead away the slap of despise and the
Kick of a husband's wrath;
And the porridge will have dropped on
The chain dress, irretrievably!
The cows will have eaten the garden crop
While you ate *acuga* fruits!
The white ants will have rained and flown
Away, while you looked for lion's tail hair
To tie your fire grass.

What is missing in me as woman?
My voice is pure and thin as a
Snail's love whistle:
When I sing as I collect wood
Sheep walk far
And goats sneeze
Cows graze with emphasis
Ears propped and then waving and the herders hum
    nonchalantly;
My voice pierces the ears of the shadows
Of the trees and rides the sun.

The disease of dogs the soldiers brought
From Ethiopia, and Burma and white women,
The disease they brought from the war
That eats and rots the womb
That makes men leak and rats eat the
Front of their trousers;

The disease the men of the town drink
From waters and eat from silver plates;
That disease of rotting that makes them
Bite their lips and stand on their toes
When they pass water,
Like they were passing out a spear
Through their third leg!
That disease which has eaten away
The fire poker from the homes of many big people
And they only "darling"
When the time comes to sleep
And they only exchange salivas.

That disease which has brought coldness
In many homes and makes the wives
Of big men
Stuff the young bulls of other people's rearing
With "want me only" herbs,
And trap from other women the power
Of their young spears,
In expensive handbags;
And to impose wears and gifts on young men,
Products of their labour of nerves
From haunts of stale overdue passions
From wives of those who have fallen into things!
Wives who want their own cars,
In the name of means of travel to club meetings,
To taxi trapped youngsters.

The women of perfume,
The women of heels in the air,
Of packed and suffocated buttocks
And of toasted hair,

And with hearts for money,
Go to Association meetings to plan the
"Cheat the Husbands Campaign".
And how to win the battle of waists
Against the young men,
And do not speak but vomit at husbands when
They ask any questions.
And the pecked husbands
Throw their venom on men of lesser rank
In the offices
And come to office with their eyes
As black as the clouds in the East!

That disease of town baptism
That eats the hair off the heads of women
And of children born in disease:
Forcing women to wear hairs of goats
And big dogs:
The disease they wrap under wears of
Many monies
Has not fouled my womb.

The way of my womb does not
Smell like a dead dog's throat
And I have no need for cosmetics to bribe stenches

Unlike the woman who throws herself about,
Fussing here, then there,
Kicking calabashes and all around
And on her path;
Doing everything all at once:
Waking up smoke from between cooking stones
Amid curses and pretended impatience;

Misplacing things and confusing herself more
Till she washes the cooking pot
With a naughty goat's urine,
Donated by the owner into a container left
Carelessly around the hut.
The woman who is everywhere as if her roof
Was leaking:
Dashing with that speed to cheat her man
From staying around the home
To catch the man who bores her secretly;
Her secret lover now dangling under the bed,
Breathing softlier than a snail!

Unlike the woman caught red-handed,
I smell of woman pure
And I have nothing to hide from men's noses.
Who has ever turned urine into honey
And which man has ever milked the cow
That grazes on the moon's pasture!
My hut knows no shame.
The hollow eyed woman of selling,
That dustbin,
That urinal for the quick ones of men
Of wet pockets;
The woman with the privacy of a
Market path and the shame of a
Sheep in moon,
The woman who will sigh-groan to
Her drunkard catch of the night
While her intestines
Struggle with illness!
Cannot finish all
The men.

The woman who brings drunkards to do
Things of shame on her children in their
Half sleeps,
Will not take all the men away.
The sun sets for the woman of money too,
And
The men know the place of bathing is
Not the place of drying the body.

I have no English for the men of
"Yes, yes, no" to marry;
When I laugh from the caves of my
Shuddering body and pedestal my
Sand polished maize seeds,
They say I howl like
The *Otara* hyena;
When I giggle and throw my neck loose
To throw my woman to the men,
I am called primitive;
When my breasts beckon and sway firmly
As I dash the briskness of
My youth like the heifer in season,
The men of English
Pocket and turn their heads
To the bush
And look at me as if I was mucus.
They say we are the seeds the June
Sun dried in the soil.
They say our toe nails tear their bed sheets
Bought in the towns and the *kwon*
Remains in our hands and we tear their shirts
And we do not wash our village bodies!
Their tongues heap insults and insults

On us,
And you have to close your ears with wax.
Men of education talk as if
They do not squat
To heap.
The girl who sang the blessing of the
Spirit of fertile wombs and
Breasts of life when we cut
Tattoos around our belly dimples
And on our waist valleys
To tickle the palms of
Our lovers;
My chief-mate in the *Akwali* dance team,
With whom we
Broke,
Then vibrated
Our
Middle and prided our succulent horns,
And sang our souls to the infectious
Chorus and the
Intoxicating spine-dissolving
Tiidi, tiiddiip, diip, bellow of drums.
My age mate now passes me by tight-lipped
Like I was a bewitched tree stump!
The playmate of my childhood with whom
We shared a termite head,
And were together as
Nose and eye,
Will not spill flat saliva
To greet me.
She will grudge me perfumed and
Dressed up greeting
In her schooled stomach;

She will not waste breath
On me
Lest a seed of her learning burst off!
My fellow in growth
Throws cereals only to the bush
Fowls
And when the fowls fly away,
The chicken will be no more to cook
For guests.
The decorator of my belly dimple
Breaks the oil calabashes
And leaves nothing for
Soothing the buttock boil
When it comes.
Many bitter salivas spat on your
Path,
Will some day bribe a path stump!
Education cannot blow out
For you the piece of grass in the eye,
And our fathers, and their fathers before,
Say
The grass in the front thatch of the hut
Is sacred.
When I leave this house
And the men refuse me.

My pod has been broken already
In this house.
The juice of my pod has spilled already
In the darkness under this hut,
And I am hollow now.
The man of this house sipped of
The first bitter foam of the *kal* beer

Of woman in me.
But I will not weep.
The eggs of the *Oro* dry season
Do not all hatch!

The man of this house has sipped
Of the juice,
But he has not broken the pot
And not finished the beer flour and the yeast.
Okello can have this home.
I came out of my mother alone.
Leaving a man has not struck leprosy on others
Before me.

a man

The sun does not laugh always!
The odour of orphans
Walks in clouds and blinds its fickle coys
From the eastern birth flames
To the western fires.
The wish of wizards persuades its warning
Lamps to drowse at duty;
The drown sob of roots evokes its thirst
In the season of growth;
And it yields to the appeals of clouds
When the thirst gasps of the roots of greens
And throats of cows and beasts of the bush
Strike the skies.
When the men of the village chase
The evil spirits to the muddy swamps
And weep in the rain dance

It winks a beckon to the rains!
But the sighs of orphans only hasten the coming of darkness.

The sun does not laugh always!
Cocks forget their beaks before the cooking
Pot has been put into the hut
When the womb of an orphan is in labour;
The shadows of the old men
Refuse food and defy the blaze
From the oldest logs;
The newly married kick fire pieces
On to their old men's fronts,
And the milk cows deny their calves
And upset the milk in the calabash
When the child of the cloudy skies
Insists release from the womb
Of better-off wish!

The smile of babies is balm
Of mothers' souls.
When people in the home toss
Raw tender smiles off little bodies,
And cuddle in soft sleep
Or fragile ailment
Their naively trusting little trunks:
Trunks laden with humanity
And life, arrived on Hazard's land,
Along the path from the Ancestors' restive gardens,
To the flames in the western marrying-ground
Of land and sky;
New humanity,
Come to shout to indifferent ears of skies,
Shout to ask why he too is around

With plants that do not speak,
With the beasts of all sizes and types of ferocity:
Multiplying things on a ridiculous pattern,
Pattern whose ending draws broods
And loss of appetites and fits of hysteria;
Shout and shout
To hear back his own echoed voice
Till the rains dutifully wash off his
Delible footprints from the path muds.

People in the home
Who toss and cuddle those little question marks,
Know the way to warm the cooking stones
And to bring sweat on the brows of mothers.
They know
Warm springs forgotten on laps in a dream
And milk bubbles returned in sudden vomit
With innocent unconcern or caring,
All are dried and wiped off
By saliva provoking scents from within huts
And the story of smoked eyes of mothers.
They know the key to the heart of mothers
Is in the laugh of babies
And in the glitter of their gazes.

But
The milky scent and unpredictable exits
Of these little ancestors
Restrains only the shadow spirit of their
Milk carriers.
The thirst of leaves pinches and wakes
Only the sap in the trunk,
In only one trunk,

And no puppy joys from the milk of satisfaction
In bowels of another,
And the front of twins waits not for
The second comer to the first air suckle.

The widow hollows her heart
On the grave side, but
Love giggles to her new man before the ants
In the ground
Have sharpened their skinning knives
And washed their hands and said their prayers
To the new meal that is her husband.

The sob of orphans hurts ears
And talks to the grass around the compound;
The inedible grasses around the hut,
Grasses that laugh in indifferent ungrateful
Celebrations,
To the food that fears the hollow eyes
And yelling ribs of the orphan boy;
While the village catechist preaches
Of the life of feasting after the earth's
Butchers have weighed your meat on scales.

He talks of the God of equal justice,
The all-loving God who demands love in
Gratitude for eloping with the mother of the
Orphan boy!
He does not say why the God he loves
And who loves him despises and rejects other mothers to elope
Only with his own mother.

When the orphan boy sears in sorrow's squeeze
And laughs at hunger's jokes,

His said God of the catechist
Laughs and belches in the land of feasting;
And the catechist talks of the joy of suffering
In the name of a belching God.
The orphan boy wrinkles his face in anger
Hearing of sermons on the love of suffering,
Suffering that breeds pots in holy cassocks.

He says a baby wills suffering orphanage,
That orphanage is not the big Gamester's JOKE,
Of the Joker playing games with us all
In the name of the civilised life hereafter;
In the name of a purpose to our
Own benefits !

He talks of *willing* lips,
Tender, hunger thinned,
Abandonly outstretched in screaming
And unseeing gaze, tear pooled;
Little hands clawing dying breasts and still
Tenderness,
Logged into helpless departure into dying;
Cold departure,
Departure silent to screams for milk:
Slumber,
Unheeding slumber into stench
Amid the music of pure screams of her baby !
The chilling melody of those screams
Cannot be willed.

okello's milk sister

We,
My orphan brother in birth
With whom we shared a mother,
With whom we drank of the same blood,
My brother and I
We are hungry and mama is gone;
And mama is gone, gone,
Gone out without a return
Before the fire she lit in the cooking place
Had caught the wood and the flames,
Had began to sing and scowl,
Feeling ripe and ready for the challenge
Of performing the pregnancy rites
Of the cooking pot.

Since things took her away long ago,
She left my brother and I,

Us,
To whips and sticks and stones
To the easy reach of hands and fingers,
Fingers and hands itching to scratch me,
To maul me,
To splash bile and smear soot
On the tender shoot in my inside;
To red and black eyes that always spoke
Of consumption,
Of hands of leprosy, with hungry jealousy
Against my being,
And of the perpetual centre of the sun, at mid-day,
Reigning in wanting and wanting to dry me inwards.

Since her light flickered their warmth
Out and away,
Hands of the woman who took over mama's husband
Have beaten drums on my chest;
And the vomits of this woman,
Of this woman who bellows
And sits there like a drunk cow,
Is all I have had for humus and
For the moulding pool of sweet illusions from mothers
For daughters;
For their clays in moulding towards raw pots,
Raw pots still firm in rawness,
Pots yet untempered through the moment of destiny
In the bonfire of initiation.

Without a mother to love you,
To pretend disgust in the sweet hollow ways
Of a proud woman in mocking
At her loved one;

To caringly mock as your groping voice
With coy courage of venturesome youth
Rises to sing in melody with the hums
Of the grinding stone and the chorus
Of laughing millet grains;
To steal looks at your unripe neck-breaking
And your waist and breast wriggling
And then palm down and away
Her joy's smiles;
To reveal her prides for herself in you
Through her loud complaints about
Many nothings.

To tell you that you will come home
Empty handed from your new clan in
Your place of marriage;
That men will pass you by
And leave you to split wood forever
In your mother's house and chew out
Her tired nipples with your aged teeth,
If your tongue urinates into the ears of men
And the men shake and turn their heads away,
Whistling out and catching their heads
As coldened hunters do when ill omen's spear
Passes them by in a narrow miss;
And if your eyes
Flash lust's tongues of fire at men,
Splashing out sparks of beckoning passion
Like October lightning.
And your eyes rape and stare across nights
Like the fires of a fire-fly in a hunt for a mate
And they refuse to sleep

And prevent you from facing the lonely cold
In sleeping alone.

Without a mother to love you,
I have had curses for teasings
And sweet longings have been replaced with fires,
Ripping fires,
Ripping and scattering forming clouds of girlhood
In me,
Searing rallying clouds in my eastern skies,
My clouds of girlhood longing for strength
Before the march of the rains ...
And before the final drizzle towards the west plains.

The woman who has replaced my mother
Says I am worthless.
She lies.
She says I am a dog not a human child.
That is her lie.
Her tongue throws out ropes and ropes of curses
And she swears with that mouth that stinks
Like that of a rhino's, her mouth
With the stench of a lion's cough;
That only men with hydrocill, with
Watery testicles that are very swollen
In between their legs,
Filling their legs
So that they walk like cows in full udders
And like people with yaws and boils
Between their bottoms ...
She lies and wizards.

I will not refuse to marry in her house
Or deny her the honour of a mother-in-law
Around the house that will marry me.
I will not stop the impostor
From reaping where she did not sow;
Nor be vindictive to the dry cruelty
And naked hatred of a wizard in her.
No.
Not me, daughter of Apio,
Because I know
She is only full of a fear:
Full of cannibalous fear; full
Like a swamp choking with mud.

She is afraid deeply
Of the rumble of the thunderstorm
That will be master of initiation
Roaring master of ceremonies
In the moment of birth of my clouds.
Afraid of the rumble of the thunder
Provoking rumbles of hooves,
Of hooves for my dowry,
Excited hooves surging and charging towards
The kraal of my father,
Cows running, and jogging and kicking out
In fits and mocks and in a melee of excitement
From the smell of the imminent rains;
Cows and goats and sheep
Waving horns and dangling udders,
Heralds coming on and on
Bringing home the message of my mother's arrogant
Triumph;
Dancing and kicking up dust and

93

Dancing the fulfilment dance
Amid bellowing and mooing
Proud *ijira* calls, and beating up *kaluulu*
To my mother's birth of a daughter.

She lies from behind that cruelty
Because I see the fear in her eyes.
I see the pride of my stubborn insides
Sear her eyeballs
And I laugh with the pride of the underdog.
I laugh with the force of the seed in me,
Of the seedling shadow in me
Pricking and talking and telling my limbs
To fight the invasion of thorns
And rodents
With deadly desires;
Wanting its sweet soft leaves just out in timid
Winkings, in a waiting.
I laugh with the power of the boiling lava
In my deeper centres,
Molten and bubbling liquids talking talks
Below the layers of the malice of this woman
Who has taken over the husband
Of mama;
Molten fires that know of the freedom in
The cool fresh airs that fill the spaces
Above the surfaces;
Hot liquids,
Liquids that are with a fire that never die;
Watery rocks that are in flames,
That are red as the insides of a lion's mouth;
Like a hungry beast in a yawn;
Hot liquids that flash out their red-hot bosoms

94

Flashing out warnings of the yearning inside the
Surface,
Yearnings to harden to a total hardness
Destined for them
In their place of liberty in the sun,
When the crust of suppression is exploded out
In the day of the final outburst.

We,
My milk brother and I
The only visible footsteps of Apio,
Our mother now gone,
Shall face the challenge of the anguish
Of self-tailoring
Of scratching beyond flat existence.

I shall bring the cows home
Dowry cows and goats and sheep,
To buy estates for a place in the open sun
For Okello's pride.
I shall drink the growls of a husband, all,
Without a drop of a grumble
Breathe in,
Latrine odours oozing out of a drunken husband,
Of my man decomposed in sodden abandon on me;
I shall roast cowhide for our meal of the night
With a husband who has no arms,
Do all,
Suffer all with the calm silence of a sheep
And patient care of a cobweb spider,
To bring the torch of freedom into the darkness
In Okello's boy-hut.

We !
The fire in our insides
Shall never be trampled out.
The hottest hell is the hell fire
Of life unrealised,
The hell of the eternal never been that
Might have been,
The hell of the born condemned to unbornness,
The hell of exhaustion shut in
Into a final inactivity.

The scorpion-bitter bite
Of mama's tongue
Shall chase us all around, unendingly,
Everywhere
Of the hell of sudden demolition and tremble
On entering the arena.

The loud smiles of her wailing shadow
We could never bear !

okello's father

Son,
I offer no pity,
No litanies, nor curses against mutilations;
No soul bleeding, for I have bled already
And died daily since mother and roots
Of my home died, went;
Bled since the drench at Baptism and play
With Sacraments, outward signs of inward
Wounds and cruel choking,
Advancing suffocation under the opium smokes
Of the witches of Europe;
Bled medals from career servants
Rich metals for money worshippers and slum escapees
Menus for Europe's over-eaters,
And leisured them to escalating and
Intensifying murders,

And inventing bombs and breathing in and out
Neurotic recklessness;
Tearing and shattering Europe's man,
Exploding his insides into husks
And petrifying his brains,
Using lies and slogans for deodorants,
To silence the yell of stenches.

I sweated and bled oils for Europe's machines
And gave her a new madness,
The madness of production and religious work,
Annihilating brains with sound and
Shrill rhythms.

Europe's propaganda and onslaughts at
My pride and core corroded my manness,
While she gloated at success and
Desecrated the sanctity of manness with
Growing expertise and awarded degrees
To its planners,
And pet-named her guilt "profits".

Orphan,
Humanness and morals were known and practised
Before you began life;
Tenderness, humility and decency
By man to man in honour of manness;
All are burnt on the altars of Isolation
And on the worship grounds of aggressive
Selfishness, when a mother dies.
The agents of Europe knew this
And killed our Mother first and did all
To expel her spirit to the rough skies.

All I ask of you is to forget talks
Of revenge,
And remove from the path of your growth
The corrosive pills of self pity
That pity in loud wails of flogged woman
And complaints of a toothless dog.

Give the injured manness in you a chance!
Feed its yearns for a healing
On the curative herb smokes of tenderness
To manness in others;
With the humility of sane tempers
And the modesty of potent husbands
Who do not reveal the sleep with their wives
But go out in silence to cultivate,
Waiting for fertility
To argue his case and hers.

Mimic no diseases in others
In the name of "catching up" or taking
"Expert" formulae and blueprints
From the Johns and Mukasas;
No husband borrows soldiers
To fertilise his wife with,
And no sane woman goes for pregnancy
From the murderer of her husband.

Imitate and fall prey to no slogans
And traps of planning bureaux,
And degreed wizards and head hunters with
Grand titles.
Stick to and defend your salvaged oases,
Oases under sieges,

And chase no beckoning lures
Of artificial mirages
And the false images in commissioned mirrors.

Listen to the wails of your mother's spirit,
Of murdered mankind,
And struggle,
Struggle through the thorns on strange pathways
Of your making;
Through the challenge of elephant grasses
And muddy swamps and unfamiliar bushes;
Fight on
To find the proper omen plants and herbs
For erecting the shrine to her spirit
In the cleansed homestead.

Do not wince from the malicious scratches,
Never weaken at your knees
For it is the remains of manness in you,
The raw arrogance
In your white eyes and glittering
Sand polished teeth from
Within careless confidence;
That the guilty, the defeated and
The false starters fear!
You are their nag of conscience and pangs
Of shame.

Do not fear the weight of their advantage
And their means, for you share their
Ownership by proxy,
And because no wizard's medicine-poisons
Are all-killing all the time,

100

Rise to the struggle for your manness
And resurrect the manness worship cult
Of your Ancestors.

Enthrone the spirit of your mother
In the new homestead,
And let the world feel
The arrogant boast of her milk,
Stubborn woman in her
Singing of the fertility of her womb through you!

Glossary

abila

a ceremonial rite to redress the balance of forces
between the individual and cosmic forces, at a
point when the cosmos seems to be winning

abir

a type of sorghum that grows above 12 feet

acuga

a vegetable with a very bitter taste; a symbol of
tribulation or the test of oneself against bitterness
in existential experiences around one.

akwali

a fond, chauvinistic identification with one's village
(the cord which connects one's psyche and being with
the human collectivity and consciousness) — akwali
being a fond abbreviation of the village name
Okwalongwen

apele

a male who lacks the attributes of a culturally
defined man e.g. courage, dash and self-assertiveness

arum

a big communal hunt across the wilderness. Because
of the terrifying isolationism and sense of exposure
(with high possibilities of sudden death away from
home) it is a challenge to participate and to come

home with a kill (hence its cultural importance for the definition of manhood and self-sufficient individualism) — a kind of self maintenance against the cosmos, without having *mama* around to defend you against the cosmic forces

awele

wild dove — a bird that bedevils human talent (its hunters).

ijira

an outburst of individual or group assertion against the cosmos of Existence by identifying with natural objects that symbolize power and successful use of power to assure one's own existence and survival. Man identifies with power in Nature to express the feeling of power he feels inside himself in his existential confrontation with nature. This outburst often takes place at times of celebrations and happiness (man's power creates the food that enables him to feel and express his being)

kalalang

a black ant that has a sting that is extremely acidic

kwon

food made from putting millet flour in boiling water and churning to create a near-hard product

ngunydeng

a type of wild cat that traps hens by opening its anus for hens to peck and poke. When a hen has dipped its head far enough in to enable a grip, the wild cat

suddenly closes its anus. It can thus drag a
heavy weight without a fight and without allowing the
hen to raise alarm. The hen suffocates fast

obia
a type of grass that has very sharp shoots at its base

okono
pumpkin — symbol of the mockery of human rashness

oro
dry season — an off-season for fertility

otara
an ugly reference to "Europeans" with colour
connotations (the root tar meaning ashen)

otwaca
an annihilative reference to another person. In a culture
in which calling a person by their name is regarded as a
sign of recognition of their existence (and hence their
worth and care for their existence), it is very painful to a
person to call him (or refer to him) as otwaca when
talking to him. The use of the word comes in a situation
of bitter conflict. It is a no-name

shea-butter
an oil (butter) from the seeds of the Yao tree

yao
a tree

Published by the East African Publishing House
Uniafric House Koinange Street P. O. Box 30571 Nairobi and
printed in letterpress by afropress ltd., Saldanha Lane
P. O. Box 30502 Nairobi